Vegetables

words by Jill McDougall
photographs by Lisa James

S0-CWP-081

Vegetables are parts of plants.

Most people eat vegetables. Our bodies need vegetables.

Some vegetables are the leaves of the plant.

Lettuce is a leafy vegetable.
Cabbage is made up of leaves, too.
Leafy vegetables are good for us.

Some vegetables are the stems
of the plant.

We eat the stem of the celery plant.
Some people eat the leaves, too.
Celery is good for us.

Some vegetables are the seeds of the plant.

Peas are seeds. A cob of corn is made up of seeds, too. Corn and peas are good for us.

Some vegetables are the flowers of the plant.

Broccoli is a flower. Cauliflower is, too. Broccoli and cauliflower are good for us.

11

Some vegetables are the fruit of the plant.

Pumpkins are the fruit of the pumpkin vine. Squash is a fruit of a plant. Pumpkins and squash are good for us.

Some vegetables are the roots
of the plant.

Carrots are root vegetables.
Turnips are root vegetables, too.
Root vegetables are good for us.

We should eat lots of vegetables to help us grow strong.